Everyone P
Sports

Aimee Popalis

Educational Media

rourkeeducationalmedia.com

Scan for Related Titles
and Teacher Resources

Teaching Focus:
Locate the color coded maps in each section. How do the color coded maps help you as you read the text? How does the color coding make a difference?

Before Reading:

Building Academic Vocabulary and Background Knowledge
Before reading a book, it is important to set the stage for your child or student by using pre-reading strategies. This will help them develop their vocabulary, increase their reading comprehension, and make connections across the curriculum.
1. *Read the title and look at the cover. Let's make predictions about what this book will be about.*
2. *Take a picture walk by talking about the pictures/photographs in the book. Implant the vocabulary as you take the picture walk. Be sure to talk about the text features such as headings, Table of Contents, glossary, bolded words, captions, charts/ diagrams, or Index.*
3. *Have students read the first page of text with you then have students read the remaining text.*
4. *Strategy Talk – use to assist students while reading.*
   - *Get your mouth ready*
   - *Look at the picture*
   - *Think…does it make sense*
   - *Think…does it look right*
   - *Think…does it sound right*
   - *Chunk it – by looking for a part you know*
5. *Read it again.*
6. *After reading the book complete the activities below.*

Content Area Vocabulary
Use glossary words in a sentence.

competitive
courts
equipment
obstacles
racket
team

After Reading:

Comprehension and Extension Activity
After reading the book, work on the following questions with your child or students in order to check their level of reading comprehension and content mastery.
1. *When playing sports do you always need to be competitive? Explain. (Asking questions)*
2. *What is the most popular piece of equipment used in most sports worldwide? (Summarize)*
3. *Why do people play sports? (Infer)*
4. *Do you play on a sports team? How do you show sportsmanship on your team? (Text to self connection)*

Extension Activity
Sports are enjoyed by many people around the world. Even though there are many different sports worldwide, many have similarities. Choose two sports from the text. How are they similar? How are they different? Create a Venn diagram to show the similarities and differences of the two sports. Which one do you like best? Why?

People all over the world play sports.

Some sports are played with a **team**. Soccer is the most popular team sport in the world. South Africa has the most soccer clubs.

Other sports, like tennis, are played alone or in pairs. Tennis is the most popular sport in Australia.

Balls are used in many sports. The ball may be hit with a bat, a **racket**, or your hand. The ball may be thrown, dribbled, or rolled.

People in China like to play basketball. In Scotland, people like to play rugby.

Some sports, like skiing and snowboarding, need special **equipment**. The United States has the most places to ski in the world.

Skiing is a way of life for many people in Norway, Switzerland, and Austria.

Some sports, like running and swimming, need no equipment. Many of the world's fastest runners come from Kenya.

People in England were the first to make swimming a **competitive** sport.

People can play sports on **courts**, fields, or ice.

In Brazil, people play beach volleyball on sand.

People like to play ice hockey on frozen ponds in Canada.

In the United States, football is played on fields. Sometimes the fields are in stadiums.

Golf is played on a course with a series of holes and **obstacles**.

Scotland and New Zealand have the most golf courses.

Professional athletes earn money competing in sports. The winner of the Tour de France bicycle race earns about a half-million dollars!

People of all abilities can play sports. Many people play wheelchair basketball in the United States, Japan, and the Netherlands.

In any sport, good sportsmanship helps everyone have fun. Playing fairly and saying "Good game!" are ways to be a good sport.

What sports do you like to play?

Photo Glossary

 **competitive** (kuhm-PET-i-tiv): A situation in which a person or team is trying to win.

 **courts** (KORTS): Big, hard, flat areas used for some sports.

 **equipment** (i-KWIP-muhnt): Tools or supplies used in a sport.

 **obstacles** (AHB-stuh-kuhlz): Things that make it difficult to do or complete something.

 **racket** (RAK-it): Oval, stringed frame with a handle used to play games.

 **team** (teem): A group of athletes working together.

Index

Show What You Know

1. If you wanted to play golf, which countries have the most courses?
2. Name three types of balls that may be used in sports.
3. Why is good sportsmanship important?

Websites to Visit

www.bam.gov/sub_physicalactivity/physicalactivity_activitycards.html

www.olympic.org/olympic-games

www.sikids.com

About the Author

Aimee Popalis is a sports fan, athlete, and coach. She loves swimming, bicycling, and running, but softball is her all-time favorite! She hopes to try surfing someday.

© 2016 Rourke Educational Media

www.rourkeeducationalmedia.com

PHOTO CREDITS: Cover: © Pixel_Pig, isitsharp; Title Page: © Christopher Futcher; Page 3: © Andrew Rich; Page 4: © Wessel du Plooy; Page 5: © microgen; Page 6: © XiXinXing; Page 7: © Paolo Bona; Page 8: © SerrNovik; Page 9: © technotr; Page 10: © Lilyana Vynogradova; Page 11: © Purdue 9394; Page 12: © muratsenel, YvanDube, Arsen Stakiv; Page 13: © Pavel L Photo and Video; Page 14: © ImagineGolf; Page 15: © Andrew Rich; Page 16: © Graeme Shannon; Page 17: © Steven Debenport; Page 18: © Radu Razvan; Page 19: © Rob van Esch; Page 20: © JLBarranco; Page 21: © Christopher Futcher

Edited by: Keli Sipperley
Cover and Interior design by: Tara Raymo

Library of Congress PCN Data

Everyone Plays Sports / Aimee Popalis
(Little World Everyone Everywhere)
ISBN (hard cover)(alk. paper) 978-1-63430-362-0
ISBN (soft cover) 978-1-63430-462-7
ISBN (e-Book) 978-1-63430-559-4
Library of Congress Control Number: 2015931699

Printed in the United States of America, Conover, North Carolina